Miley Ray Cyrus

The Little Girl Who Grew Into A Woman

Marlow Martin

Like Britney and Hilary who came before her, Miley Cyrus has broken her squeaky-clean Disney image and transformed into an outspoken, full-fledged and often-controversial pop star. She can't stop ... putting on a *major* show! Miley Cyrus shows off her crop top-ready abs (and powerhouse vocals.)

Miley ray Cyrus "The Little Girl Who Grew Into A Woman"

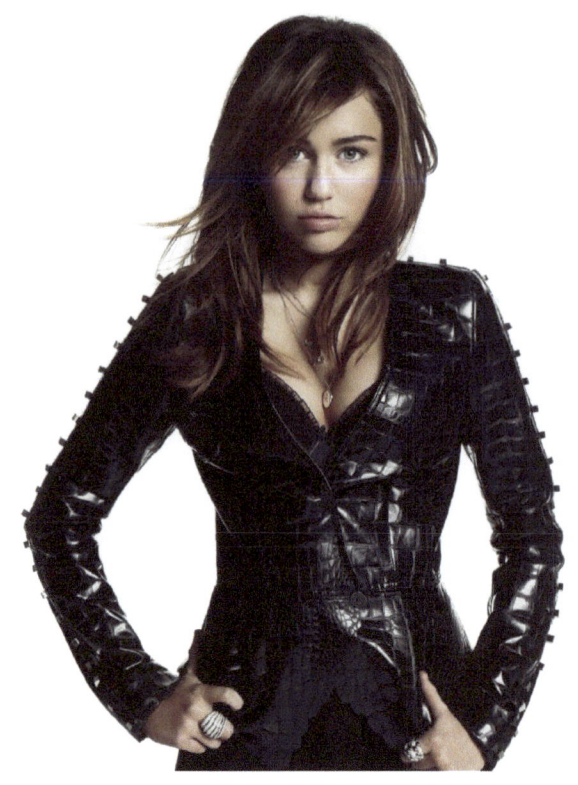

Miley Ray Cyrus is an American actress and recording artist. The daughter of country singer Billy Ray Cyrus, she held minor roles in the television series Doc and the film Big Fish in her childhood.

Born: November 23, 1992 (age 21), Franklin, Tennessee, USA

Height: 5' 4" (1.64m)

Parents: Tish Cyrus, Billy Ray Cyrus

Can't Be Tamed is the third studio album by American recording artist Miley Cyrus, released on June 18, 2010, by Hollywood Records; it would become her final album with the label after signing with RCA Records in 2013. Cyrus began planning the project in 2009, while travelling internationally for her Wonder World Tour, and continued into 2010. Described by Cyrus as a "good [record] to blast in your car", *Can't Be Tamed* represents a musical departure from her earlier work, which she had grown to feel uninspired by. As executive producers, Tish Cyrus and Jason Morey enlisted partners including Devrim Karaoglu, Marek Pompetzki, Rock Mafia, and John Shanks to achieve Cyrus' desired new sound. Their efforts resulted in a primarily dance-pop record, which Cyrus' record label acknowledged differed from the original plans for the project. Its lyrical themes revolve largely around breaking free of constraints and expectations, which are largely mentioned in the context of romantic relationships.

Upon its release, *Can't Be Tamed* received generally mixed reviews from music critics, who were ambivalent towards perceived lack of musical focus and a failure to fully establish Cyrus' maturing public image; additional criticism was placed on her vocals sounding over-processed and lacking emotional depth. It debuted at number three on the U.S. *Billboard* 200 with first-week sales of 102,000 copies. In doing so, it became Cyrus' lowest-peaking and lowest-selling record in the United States. As of January 2014, it has sold 350,000 copies in the country. *Can't Be Tamed* charted moderately on record charts in internationally, reaching the top-ten in countries including Australia, Canada, and the United Kingdom.

Two singles were released from *Can't Be Tamed*. Its title track "Can't Be Tamed" was released on May 14, 2010, and peaked at number eight on the U.S. *Billboard* Hot 100, and performed moderately worldwide. Follow-up single "Who Owns My Heart" was only released in selected European countries, failing to chart on the *Billboard* Hot 100 and charting poorly on European singles charts. Promotional efforts for *Can't Be Tamed* began to associate Cyrus with an increasingly provocative image, an effort continued with her fourth studio album *Bangerz* (2013). The record was primarily promoted through a series of television appearances and Cyrus' headlining Gypsy Heart Tour in 2011.

Background and production

"I want to do my last pop record. I'm working on a record right now. I kind of want this to be my last record for a little while and be able to take a break and just get all the types of music that I really love ... you know, my favorite styles, because in a few years, as I grow up, so will my fans, and I won't have to focus on that as much, and I'll be able to have more of the sound of music that I'm into."

— Cyrus describing the artistic transition she experienced during the production of *Can't Be Tamed*.

In December 2009, Cyrus announced that she had begun planning her third studio album and intended to begin a musical hiatus after its completion. She expressed concerns that her newer material "doesn't truly inspire me" and worried that should would be "blending in with everyone else",although she later commented that the final product was inspired by techno music qualities commonly used by recording artist Lady Gaga. Abby Konowitch from Cyrus' label Hollywood Records admitted that the record drew more inspiration from dance-pop music than she originally intended, but maintained that it "feels very comfortable for her, and it feels very comfortable in terms of the state of contemporary music."

The majority of *Can't Be Tamed* was recorded abroad during Cyrus' her headlining Wonder World Tour in 2009 and 2010. She collaborated with John Shanks during its production; he frequently traveled to London for Cyrus' recording sessions, and returned to Los Angeles to finalize their material. Cyrus also collaborated with the production team Rock Mafia, consisting of Antonina Armato and Tim James; they notably produced her earlier singles "See You Again" and "7 Things" from her first and second studio albums *Meet Miley Cyrus* (2007) and *Breakout* (2008), respectively. Cyrus stated that *Can't Be Tamed* contained a variety of dance beats and synths, but believed that its sound was secondary to the personal lyrics therein.

Release and artwork

In February 2010, Cyrus announced that her then-untitled third studio album would be released later that summer, which she felt was appropriate because it is "good to blast in your car." Later that April, it was announced that the record would be titled *Can't Be Tamed*, and would be released on June 22, 2010 in the United States. Consequently, it became the first project from Hollywood Records to be released under the "day-and-date" format, which allowed the project to be released nearly simultaneously worldwide instead of traditionally "staggering" its launch to accommodate "the availability of the artist" internationally. On May 7, Cyrus unveiled the album artwork through her website; it depicts Cyrus dressed in a leather jacket, pants, and midriff-baring shirt while standing against a black-and-white background. It was noted for establishing an increasingly-provocative public image for Cyrus; her stylist Simone Harouche stated that it was inspired by singer Joan Jett and the band Blondie, and was "basically a strong statement saying in the most simple way, that she can't be tamed–literally and metaphorically." A deluxe version of the record was simultaneously released, which included the audio disc packaged with the standard version in addition to a bonus DVD that includes previously-unseen footage from Cyrus' performance at The O2 Arena during the Wonder World Tour.

Composition

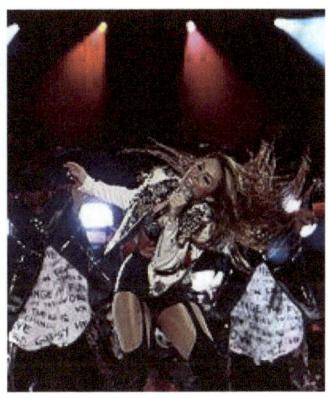

Cyrus performing during the Gypsy Heart Tour, 2011.

Can't Be Tamed is primarily a dance-pop record; it contains "several bass-heavy, slickly produced dance numbers" that Ann Donahue from *Billboard* joked "thunder in such a catchy, accessible way that it may make Kesha down another bottle of Jack out of envy." Its opening track "Liberty Walk" describes an individual who leaves a harmful relationship, which Cyrus felt leaned towards more meaningful lyrical content instead of the "super shallow" current mainstream music. "Who Owns My Heart" details the excitement in possibly finding a lover at a nightclub, while Cyrus herself commented that the title track "Can't Be Tamed" bears a theme of "breaking out and feeling free."[11] It is followed by a cover version of "Every Rose Has Its Thorn", originally performed by the band Poison for their second studio album *Open Up and Say... Ahh!* (1988); she stated that the modern-day music industry "shelters kids [from] songs as honest and real as this one", and added that a consultation with the band's lead singer Bret

Michaels helped her to incorporate her "own flare and edge".

"Two More Lonely People" was described by Evan Sawdey of PopMatters as "one moment of carefree dance-pop joy" that was reminiscent of material from her earlier *Hannah Montana* soundtracks; he also stated that the lyrics delivered in "Forgiveness and Love" were among the "more over-the-top cutesy moments" throughout the record, specifically commenting that the lines "The only thing that / Our hearts are made of / Are the acts of forgiveness and love" were "so unbelievably saccharine that Hallmark would ultimately have to turn them down".Robert Ham from *Christianity Today* felt that "Permanent December" discussed the story of "the devoted girlfriend pushing aside the 'sexy boys' vying for her affections", while "Stay" addressed the difficulties in maintaining a long-distance relationship.

Writing for AllMusic, Heather Phares noted that "Scars" exemplified Cyrus' equating of "grown-up with joyless", adding that the track fails to find the "emotional depth" Cyrus was likely intending. She also described "Take Me Along" as one of the more "overwrought ballads" where Cyrus' delivery seemed more comfortable than others on the record. Leah Greenblatt from *Entertainment Weekly* felt that "Robot" highlighted the theme of defiance and rebellion seen throughout *Can't Be Tamed*, specifically noting the lyrics "Stand here, sell this, and hit your mark / I would scream but I'm just this hollow shell".The record closes with the twelfth track "My Heart Beats for Love", which according to Ham, describes "the more universal ideal of love for all"; Greenblatt also recognized the integration of organ instrumentation.

Singles and promotion

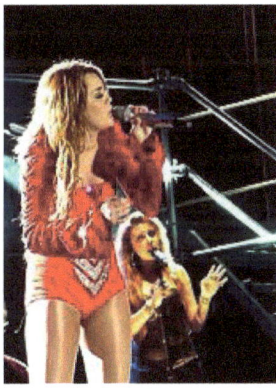

Cyrus performing during her Gypsy Heart Tour in São Paulo, 2011.

"Can't Be Tamed" was released as the lead single from *Can't Be Tamed* on May 14, 2010. It received generally favorable reviews from music critics, who appreciated its electropop influences. The track debuted at number eight on the U.S. *Billboard* Hot 100 with first-week digital downloads of 191,000 copies, although it performed moderately internationally. An accompanying music video for the song was directed by Robert Hales, and was premiered through *E! News* on May 4, 2010. It follows Cyrus and her back-up dancers dressed in bird-like clothing as they escape a cage and trash a museum. "Who Owns My Heart" was released as the second and final single from *Can't Be*

Tamed later that year. It generated mixed reviews from music critics, who felt that its production was generic. It did not impact the *Billboard* Hot 100, and reached the lower ends of European record charts. The accompanying music video for the track was also directed by Hales, and was released on October 20, 2010.

Hollywood Records focused on television appearances when further promoting *Can't Be Tamed*, which they expected would accommodate Cyrus' schedule more effectively than traditional interviews with the press and radio stations. She first performed "Can't Be Tamed" on May 18, 2010 during the tenth season of *Dancing with the Stars* in the United States. Cyrus later traveled to Europe to perform at the Rock in Rio concert in Lisbon on May 29; she was dressed in a "corset-style costume" with a "studded leather jacket and towering peep-toe shoe boots", while the performance itself was noted for painting Cyrus in an increasingly provocative light. Cyrus later generated controversy during a performance on an episode of *Britain's Got Talent* in June, where she pretended to kiss one of her female backup dancers.

On June 16, Cyrus returned to the United States to perform at the House of Blues in Los Angeles. Her performance was later re-broadcast by MTV through thirty of its international websites, reaching approximately 160 countries; it was made available for on-demand streaming the following day. Later that month, Cyrus performed "Can't Be Tamed" during the 2010 MuchMusic Video Awards, and sang "Every Rose Has Its Thorn" with Bret Michaels on *Good Morning America*. In November, she performed "Forgiveness and Love" during the American Music Awards of 2010. Cyrus launched her headlining Gypsy Heart Tour in April 2011, for which she traveled internationally.

Critical reception

At Metacritic, which assigns a normalized rating out of 100 to reviews from mainstream critics, *Can't Be Tamed* received an average score of 48, which indicates "mixed or average reviews", based on nine reviews. A writer for *Us Weekly* provided a favorable review, opining that Cyrus successfully transitioned from the juvenile public image she cultivated with her television series *Hannah Montana*; however, they criticized the "overproduction" seen throughout the project, which "can't mask her thin voice".Heather Phares from AllMusic shared a similar sentiment in regards to its production, suggesting that the excessive use of Auto-Tune limited Cyrus' ability to express genuine emotion, adding that several tracks were similar to "Tik Tok" by Kesha "minus that song's mindless fun". A writer for *Billboard* also noted Cyrus' a lack of emotion in Cyrus' vocals, but considered the "delightfully robo-country" cover version of "Every Rose Has Its Thorn" as the standout track from the record.

Writing for *The Boston Globe*, James Reed questioned the need to "tame" Cyrus, given that "this stuff is already pretty innocuous". However, he acknowledged that *Can't Be Tamed* contained "the catchiest Top 40 hits money can buy." Referencing the lyrics in "Every Rose Has Its Thorn", Leah Greenblatt from *Entertainment Weekly* felt that Cyrus was "just not (yet) that thorny a girl" despite visible efforts of rebellion. Alexis Petridis of *The Guardian* thought that Cyrus lost sight of her target audience with the project, noting that "if you're old enough to stay up after 9:00 PM without asking permission, it's not intended for you" while also commenting that children that may be interested in the record had likely "transferred their affections" to the then-teenage Justin Bieber. Writing for *Rolling Stone*, Rob Sheffield opined that the production used throughout *Can't Be Tamed* felt too generic for its goal of rebellion.

Theon Weber of *The Village Voice* felt that Cyrus' attempts of maturity were too similar to those of Christina Aguilera and Britney Spears in their earlier years, and commented that the album itself was "sadly wan". Evan Sawdey from PopMatters shared the same concern, additionally noting the irony that Cyrus' first project after *Hannah Montana* was released through the Disney-owned Hollywood Records. Elysa Gardner from *USA Today* opined that Cyrus had successfully "made the full leap from tween queen to pop tart" with the music video for "Can't Be Tamed", but failed to maintain this image with "generic, anonymous tunes" on the parent album.

Commercial performance

In the United States, *Can't Be Tamed* debuted at number three on the *Billboard* 200 with first-week sales of 102,000 copies, behind the 741,000 and 157,000 units moved by *Recovery* by Eminem and *Thank Me Later* by Drake, respectively. The record was viewed as a commercial disappointment in the country, given that Cyrus' second studio album *Breakout* (2008) debuted at number one on the chart with first-week sales of 371,000 copies. As of January 2014, the album has moved 350,000 units in the United States. *Can't Be Tamed* reached number two on the Canadian Albums Chart, and peaked at number ten on the Top 100 Mexico.

Can't Be Tamed performed moderately on national record charts in Europe. It peaked at number one on the Spanish PROMUSICAE, and reached the top-five on the Ö3 Austria Top 40, German Media Control Charts, Greek IFPI, Hungarian MAHASZ, Irish IRMA, Italian FIMI, and Swiss Hitparade. Furthermore, the record peaked in the top-ten on the Flanders and Wallonia regions of the Belgian Ultratop, Norwegian VG-lista, and the UK Albums Chart. In the latter country, the album was certified silver by the British Phonographic Industry. *Can't Be Tamed* charted in the lower ends of the Danish Tracklisten, Dutch MegaCharts, The Official Finnish Charts, French SNEP, and the Swedish Sverigetopplistan. It did, however, attain a gold certification in Poland. In Oceania, *Can't Be Tamed* peaked at numbers two and four on the Official New Zealand Music Chart and the Australian ARIA Charts, respectively. In the latter nation, it was recognized with a gold certification.

Miley ray Cyrus "The Little Girl Who Grew Into A Woman"

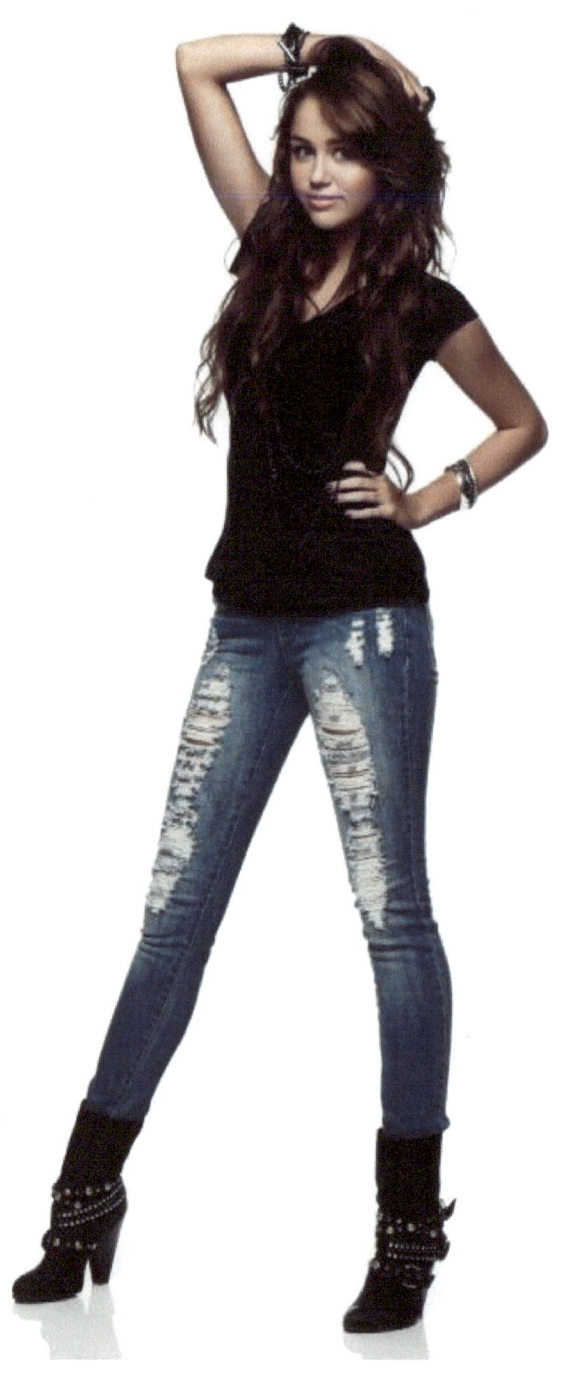

Miley ray Cyrus "The Little Girl Who Grew Into A Woman"

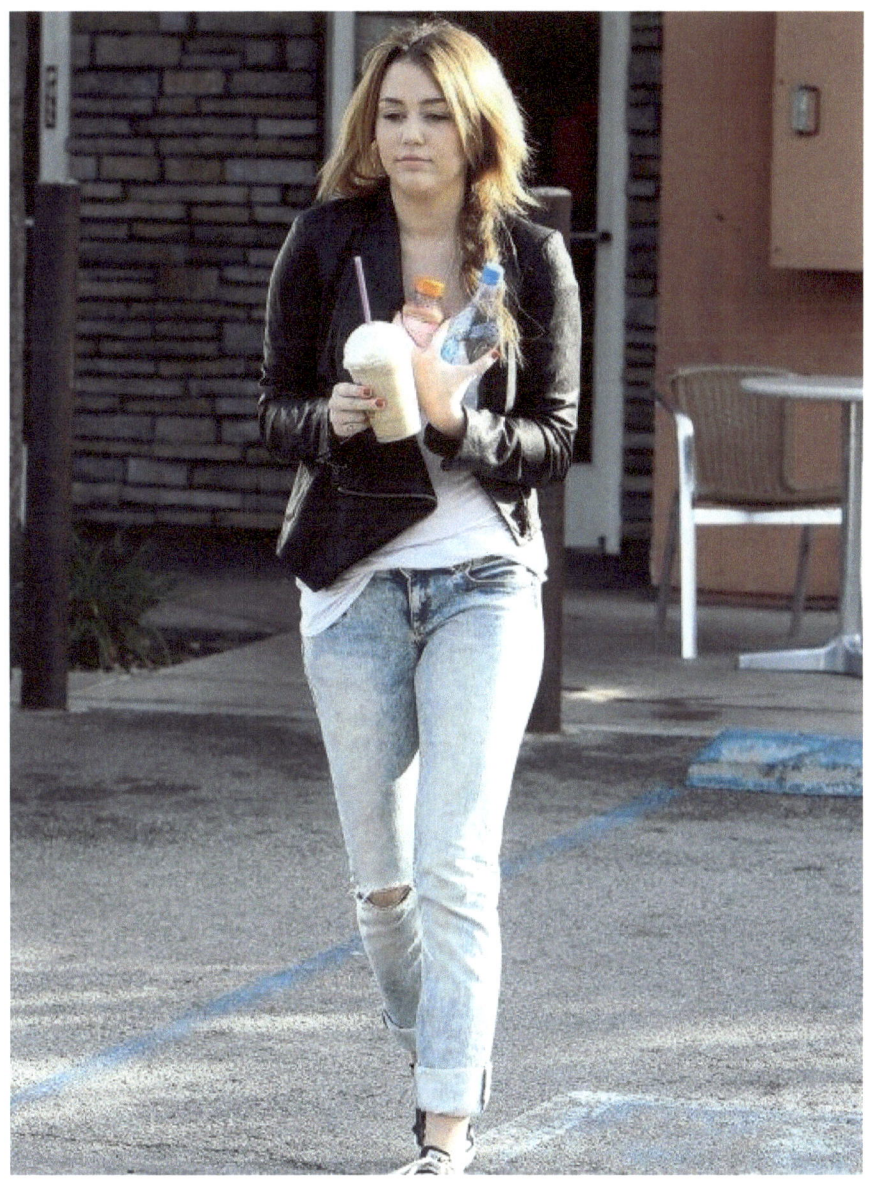

Miley ray Cyrus "The Little Girl Who Grew Into A Woman"

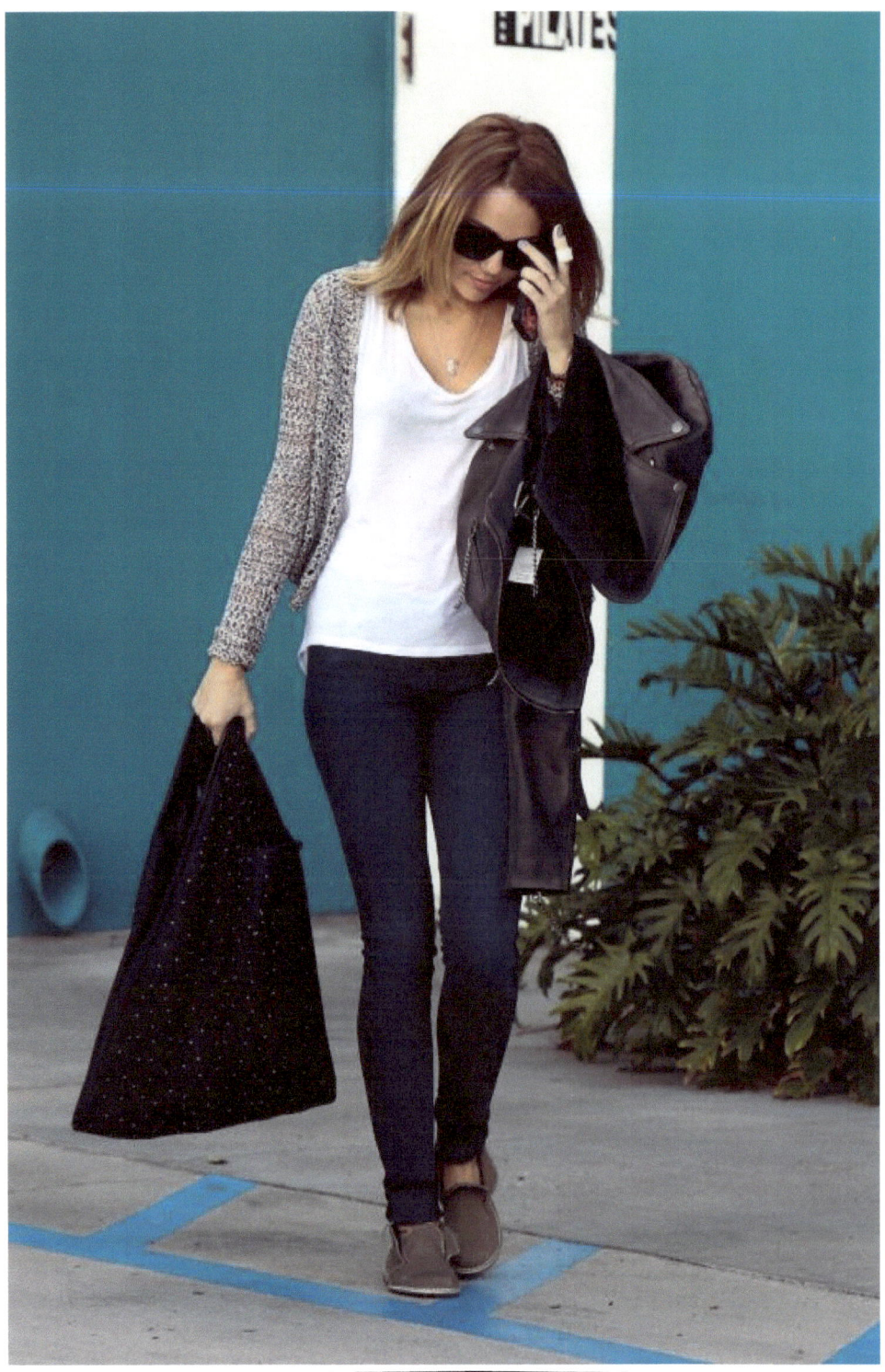

Miley ray Cyrus "The Little Girl Who Grew Into A Woman"

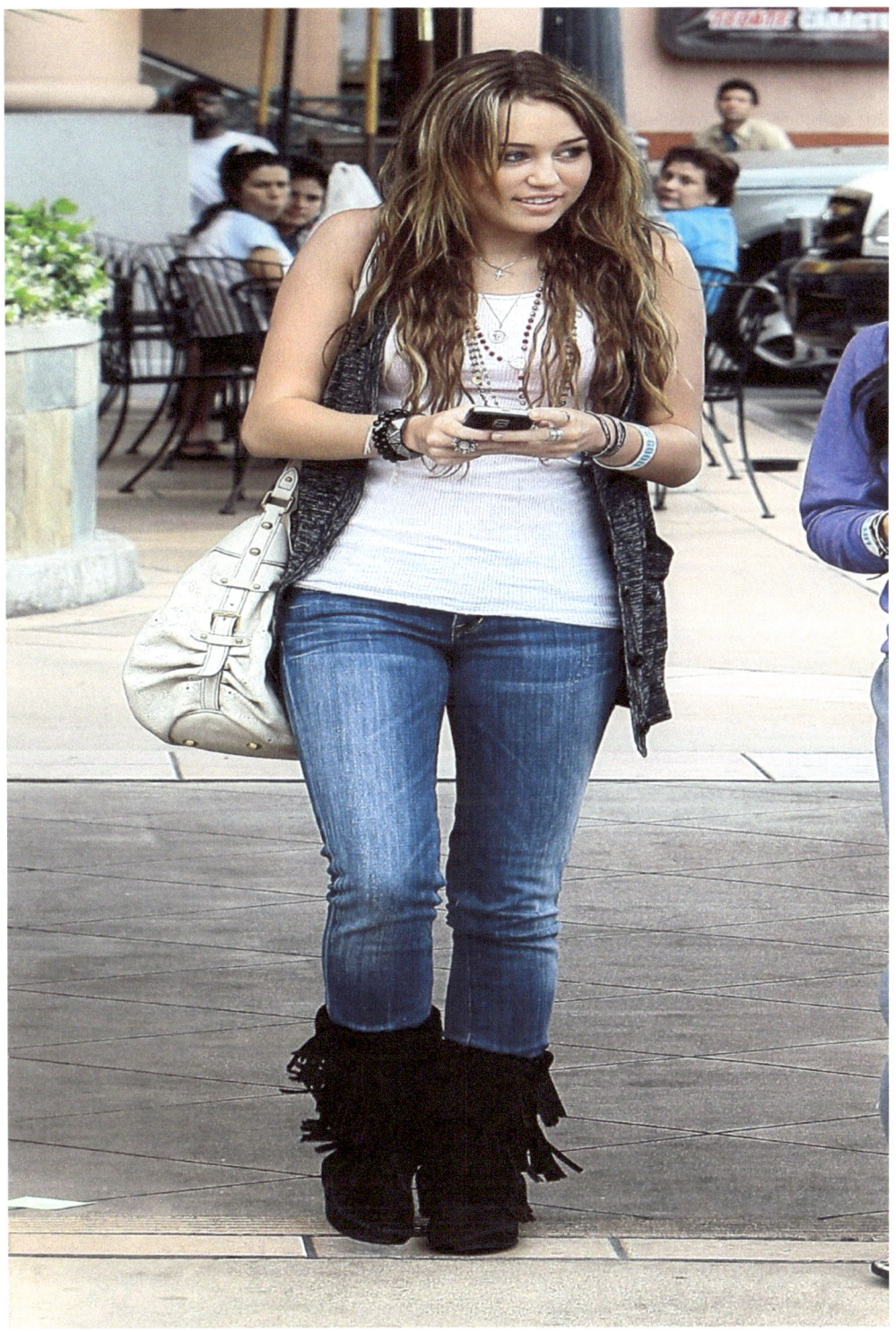

Miley ray Cyrus "The Little Girl Who Grew Into A Woman"

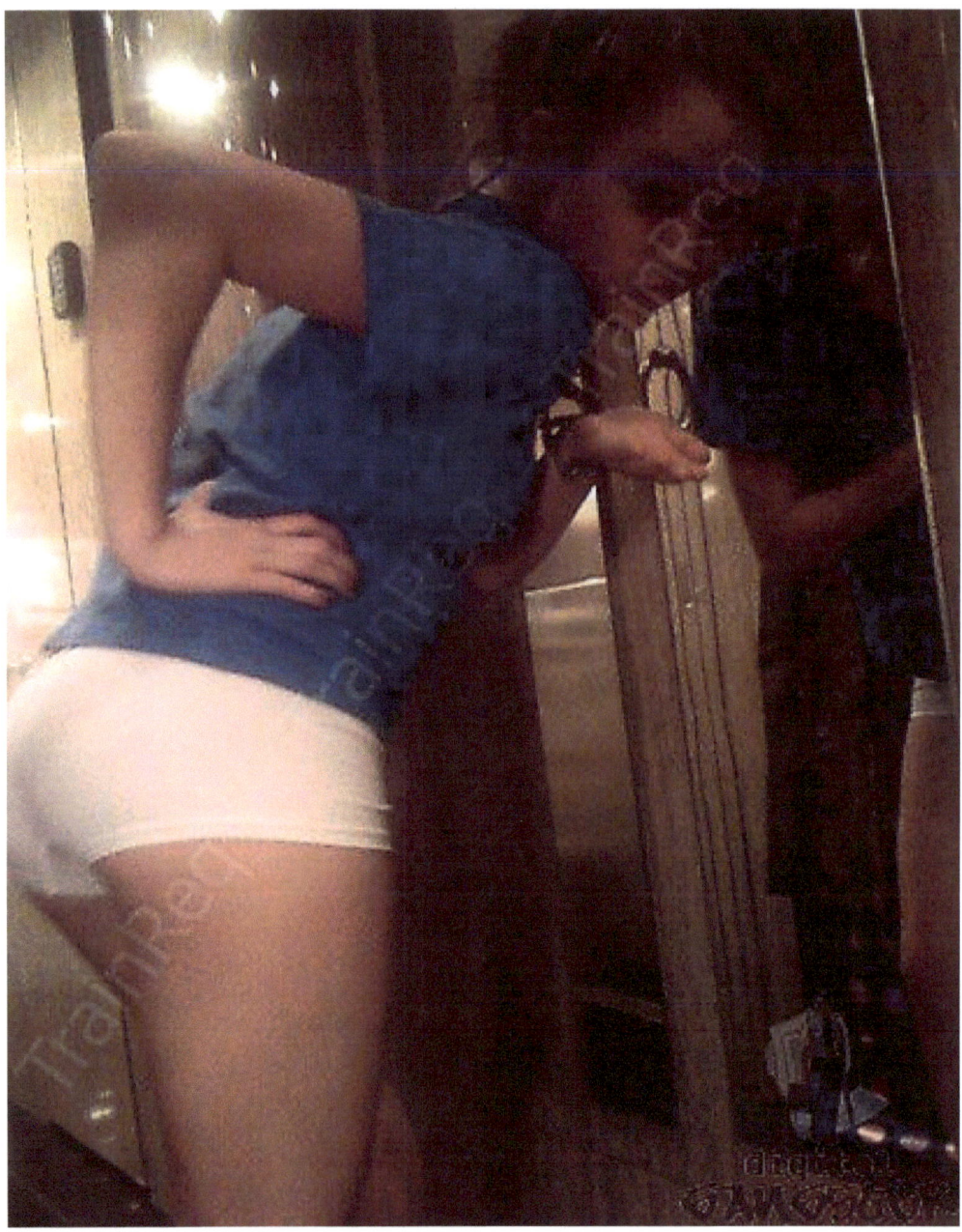

Miley ray Cyrus "The Little Girl Who Grew Into A Woman"

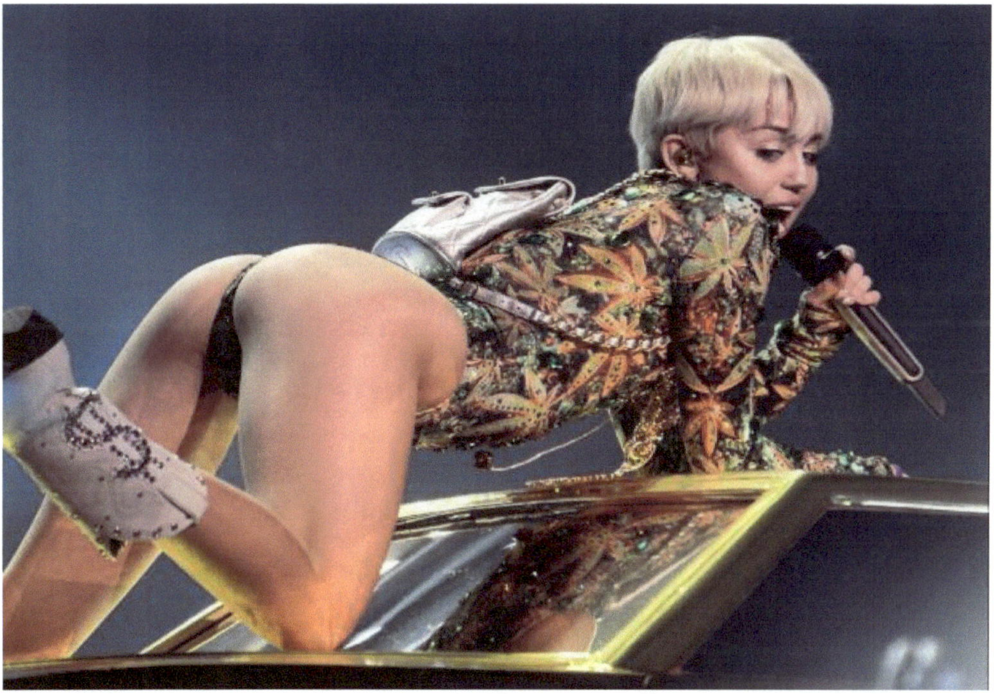

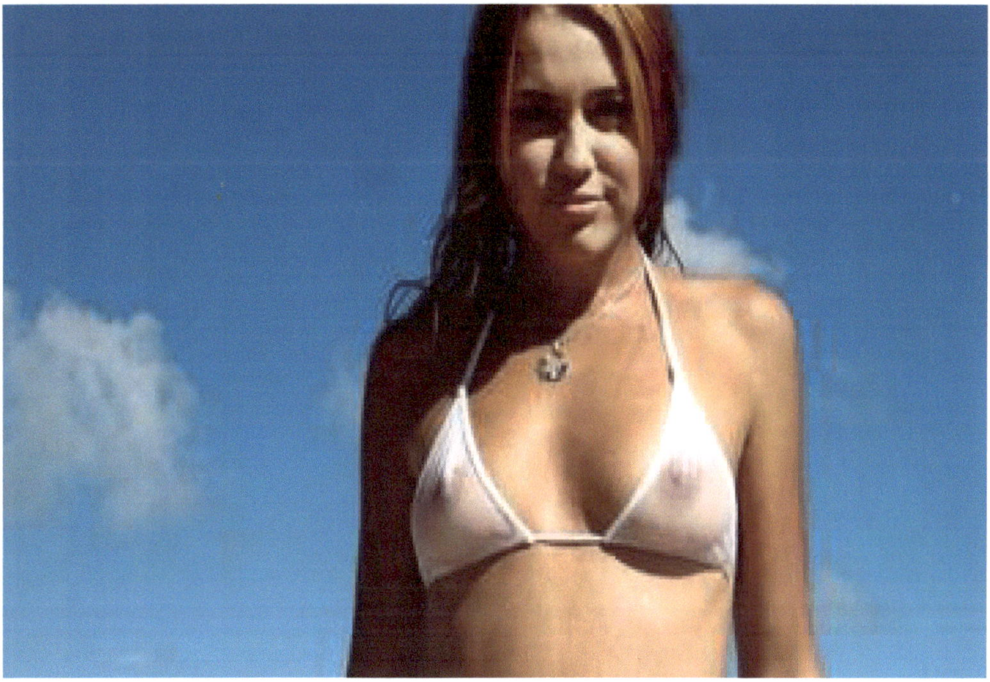

Miley ray Cyrus "The Little Girl Who Grew Into A Woman"

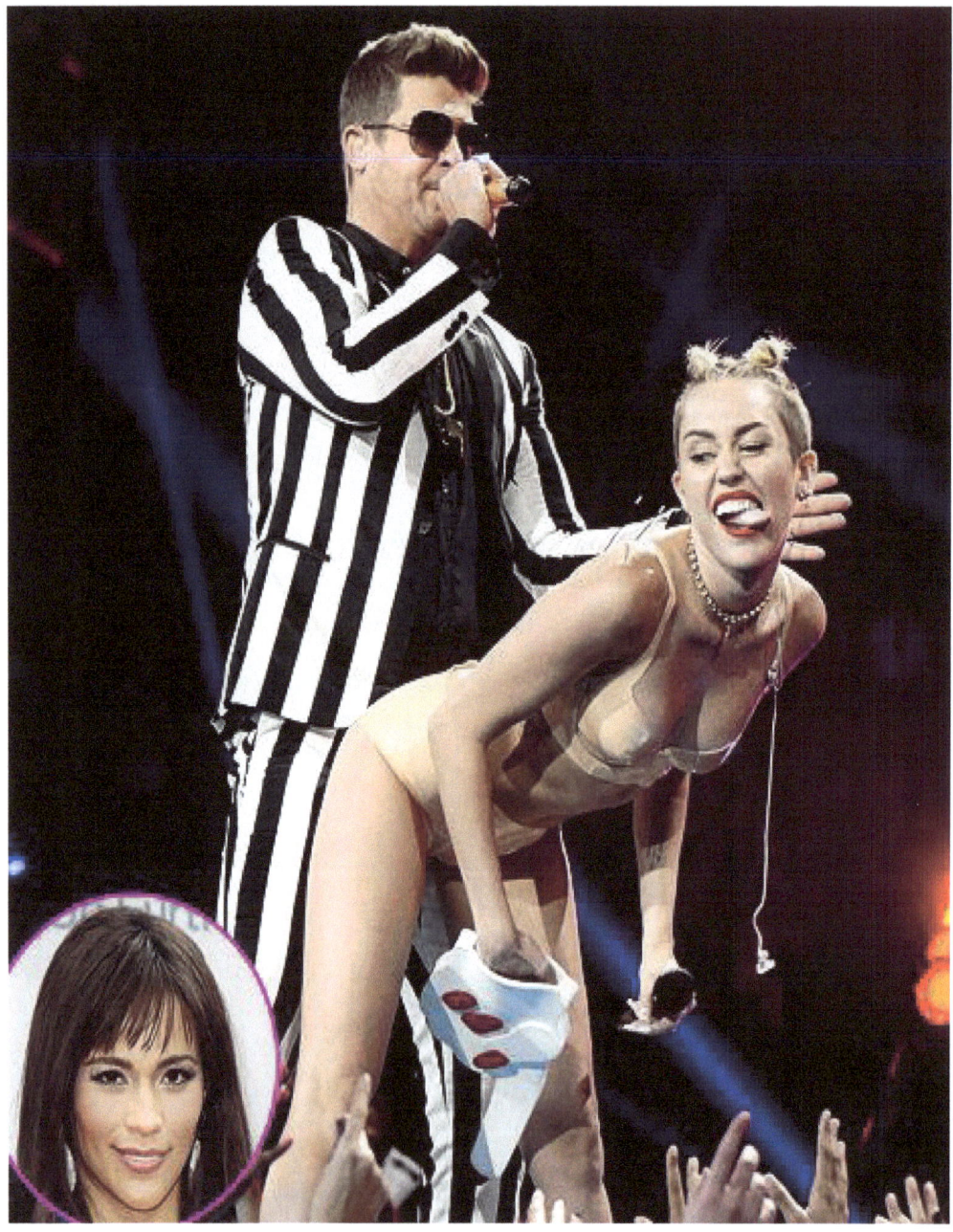

Miley ray Cyrus "The Little Girl Who Grew Into A Woman"

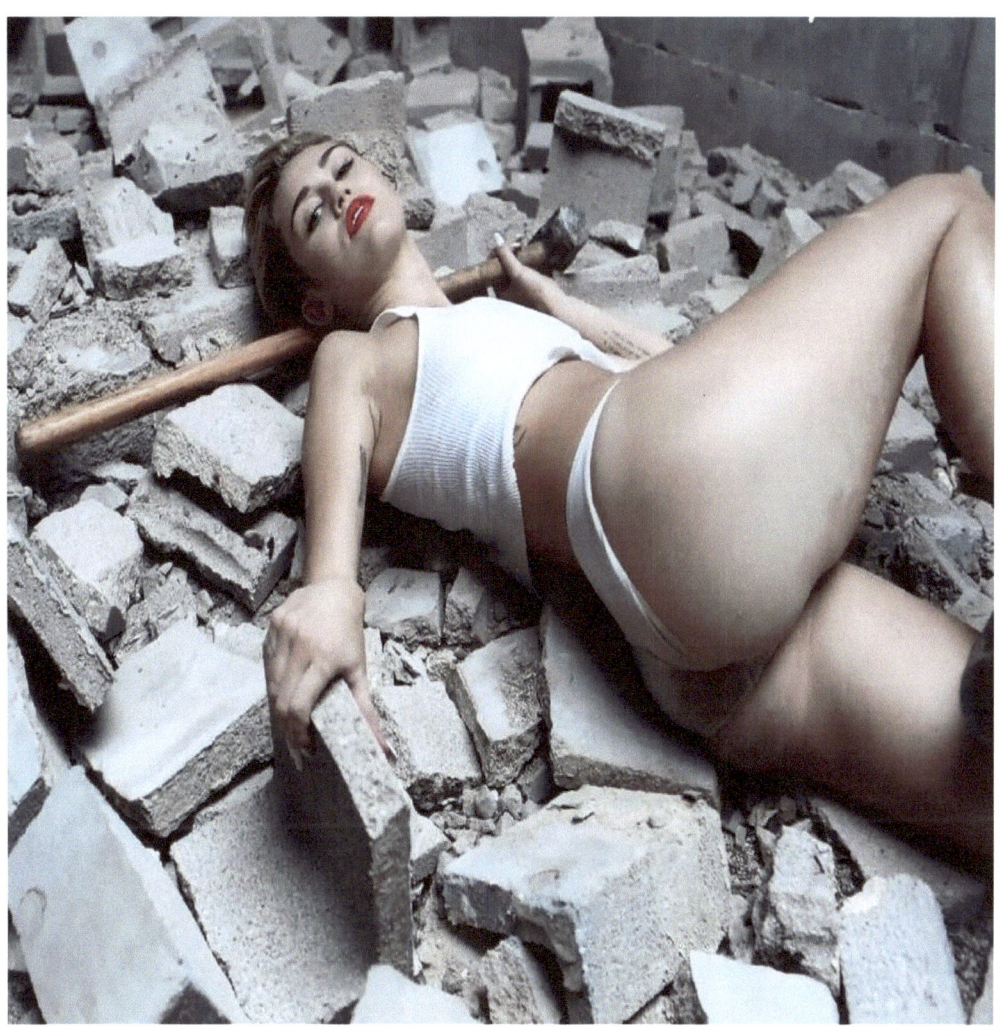

Sexy Picture

Miley ray Cyrus "The Little Girl Who Grew Into A Woman"

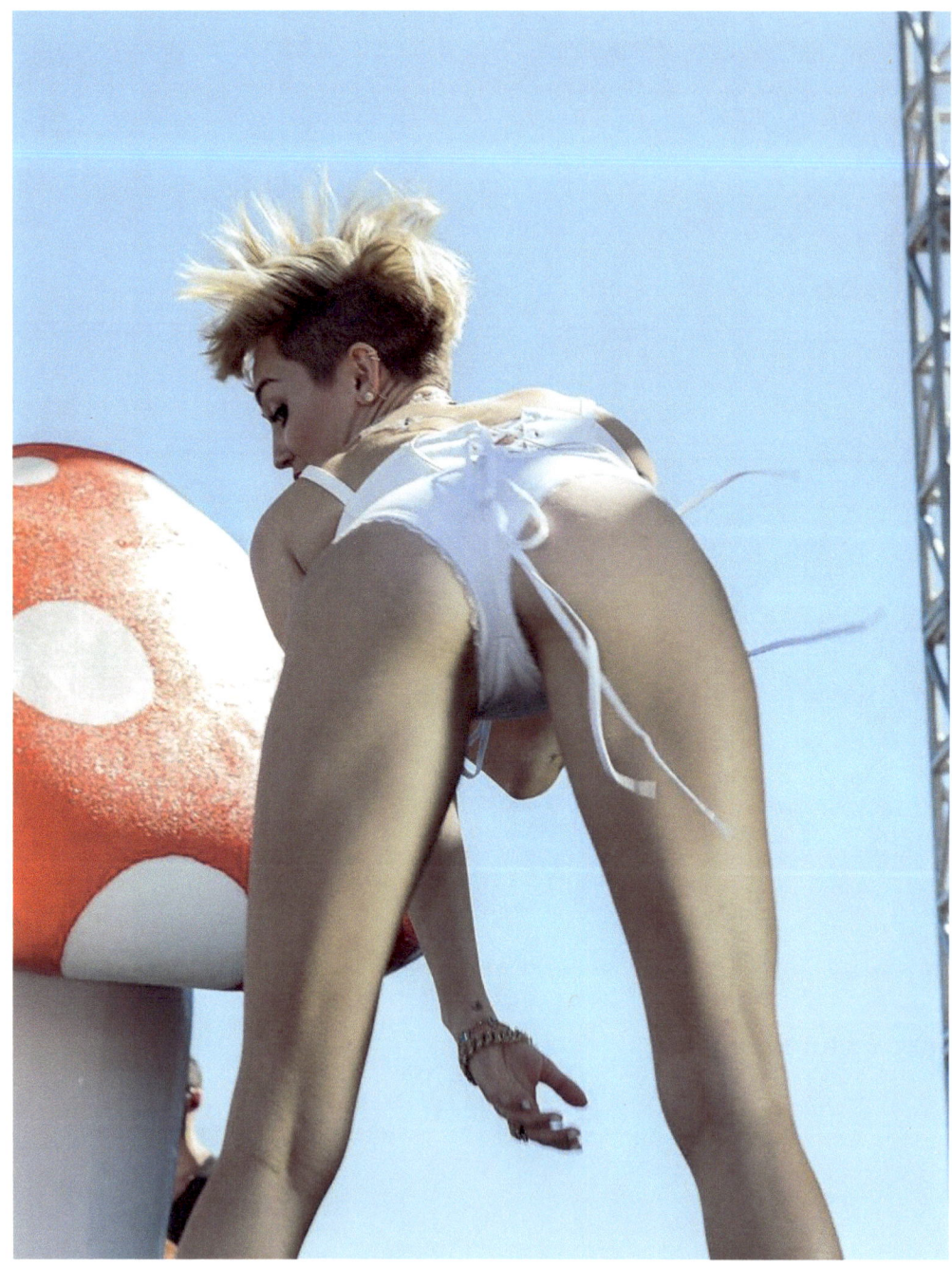

Miley ray Cyrus "The Little Girl Who Grew Into A Woman"

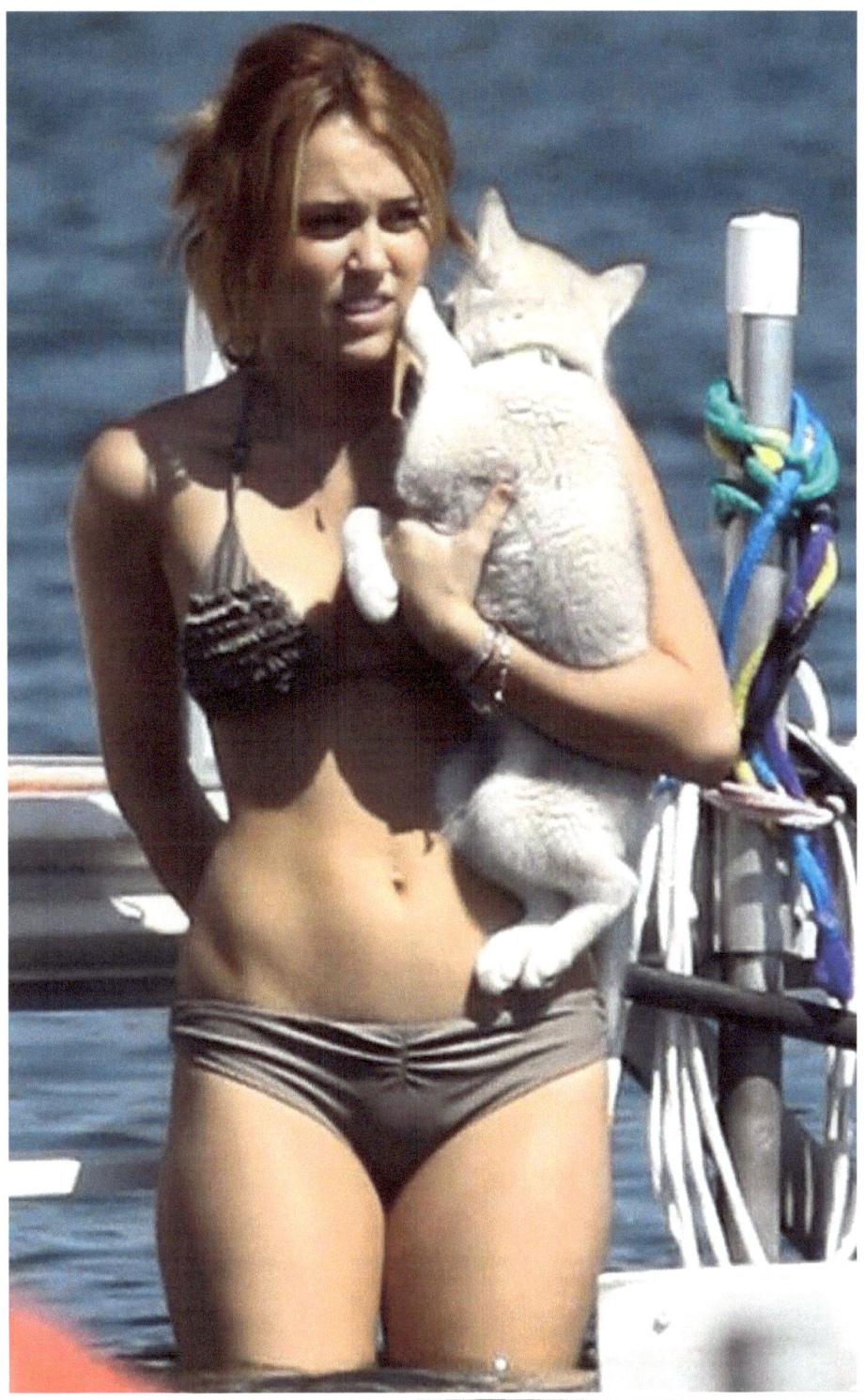

Miley ray Cyrus "The Little Girl Who Grew Into A Woman"

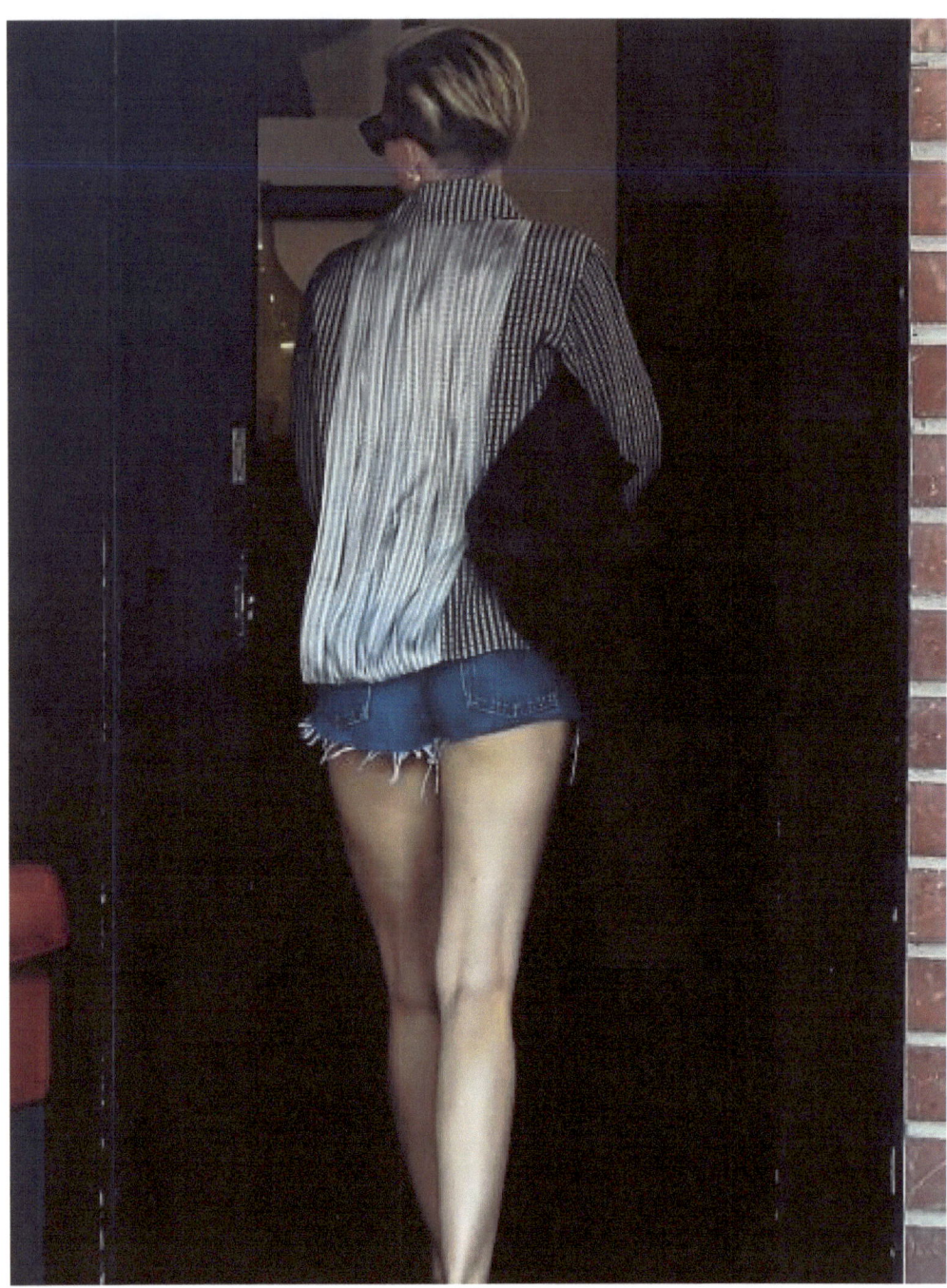

Miley ray Cyrus "The Little Girl Who Grew Into A Woman"

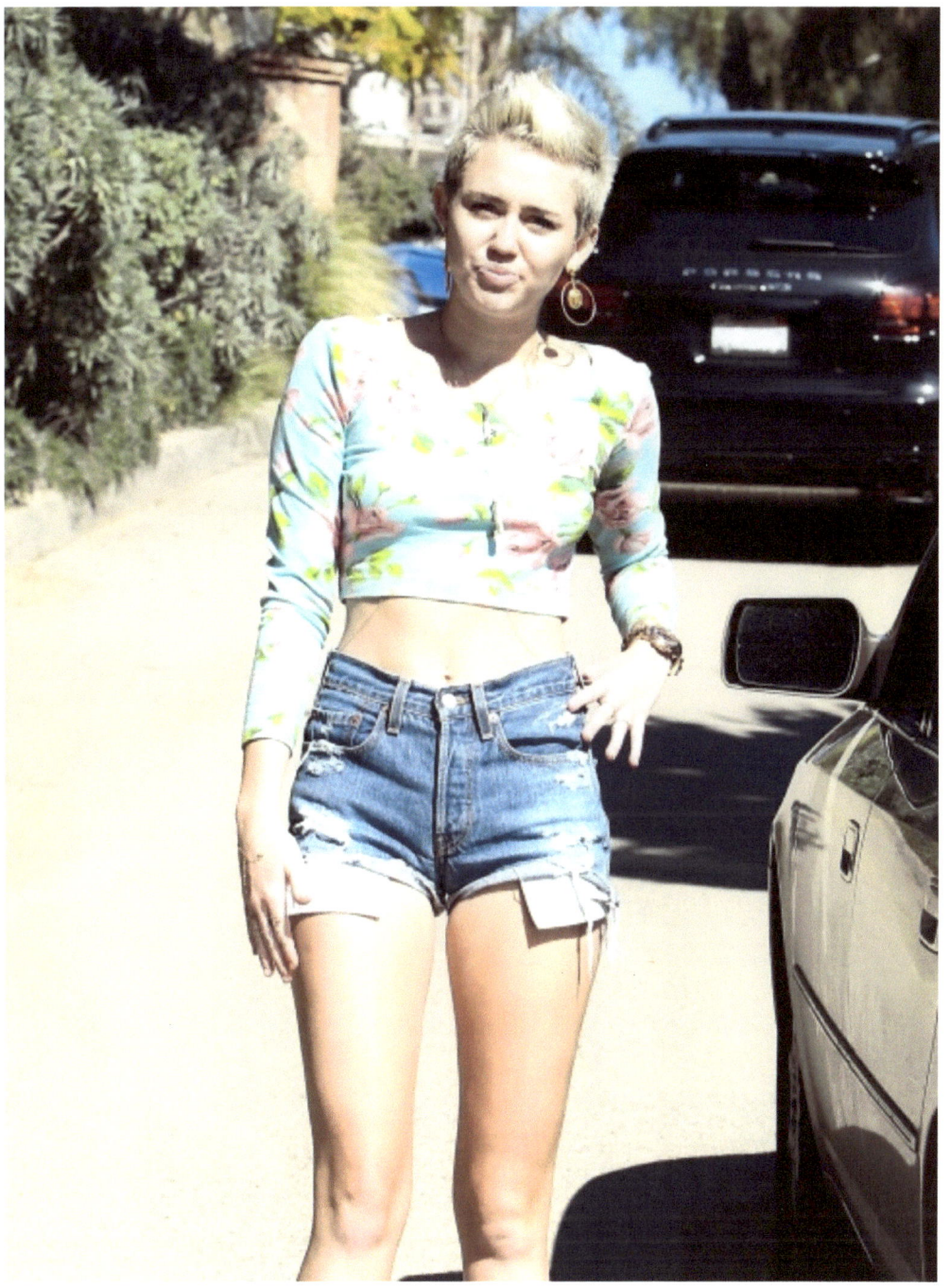

Miley ray Cyrus "The Little Girl Who Grew Into A Woman"

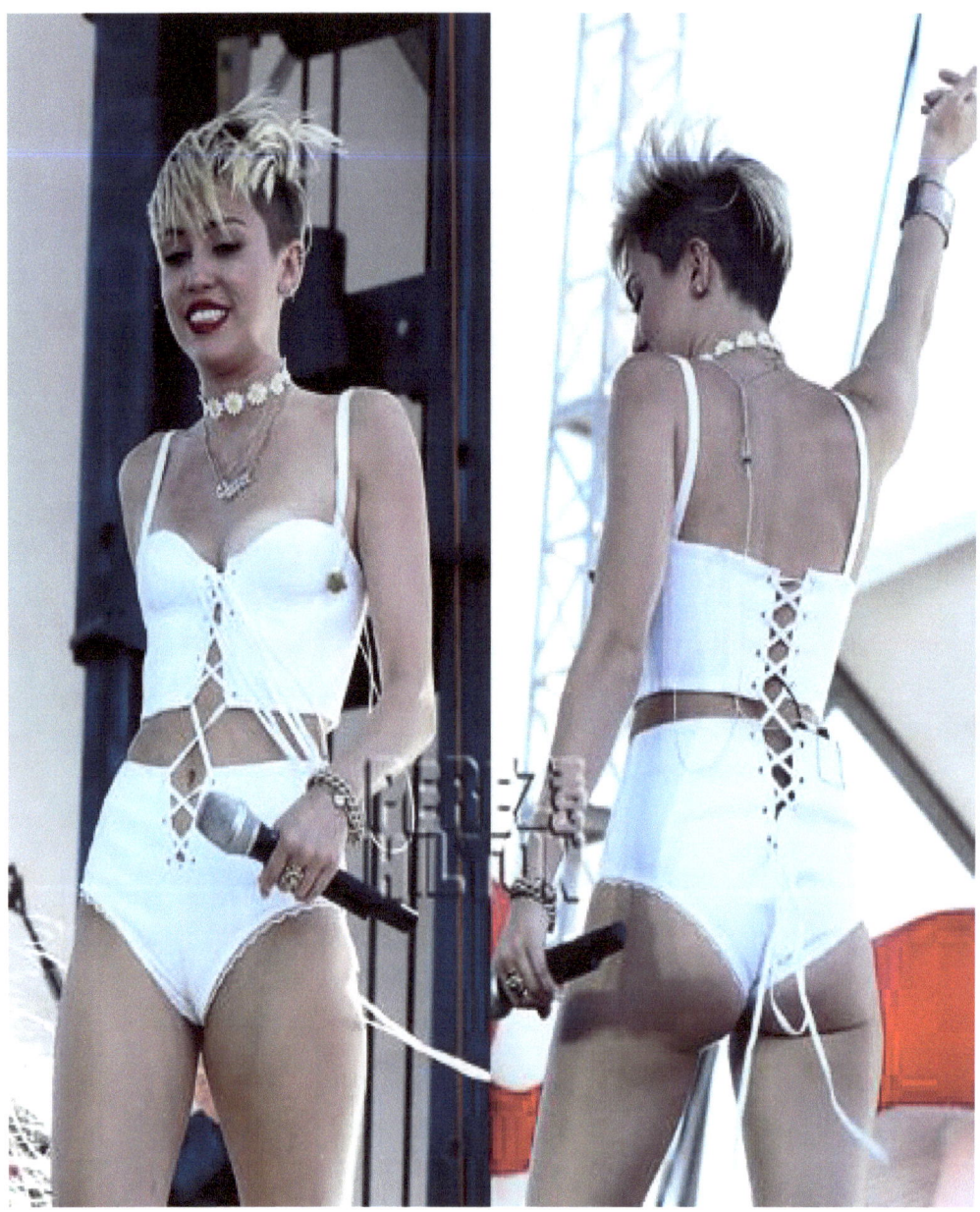

Sexy!!

Miley ray Cyrus "The Little Girl Who Grew Into A Woman"

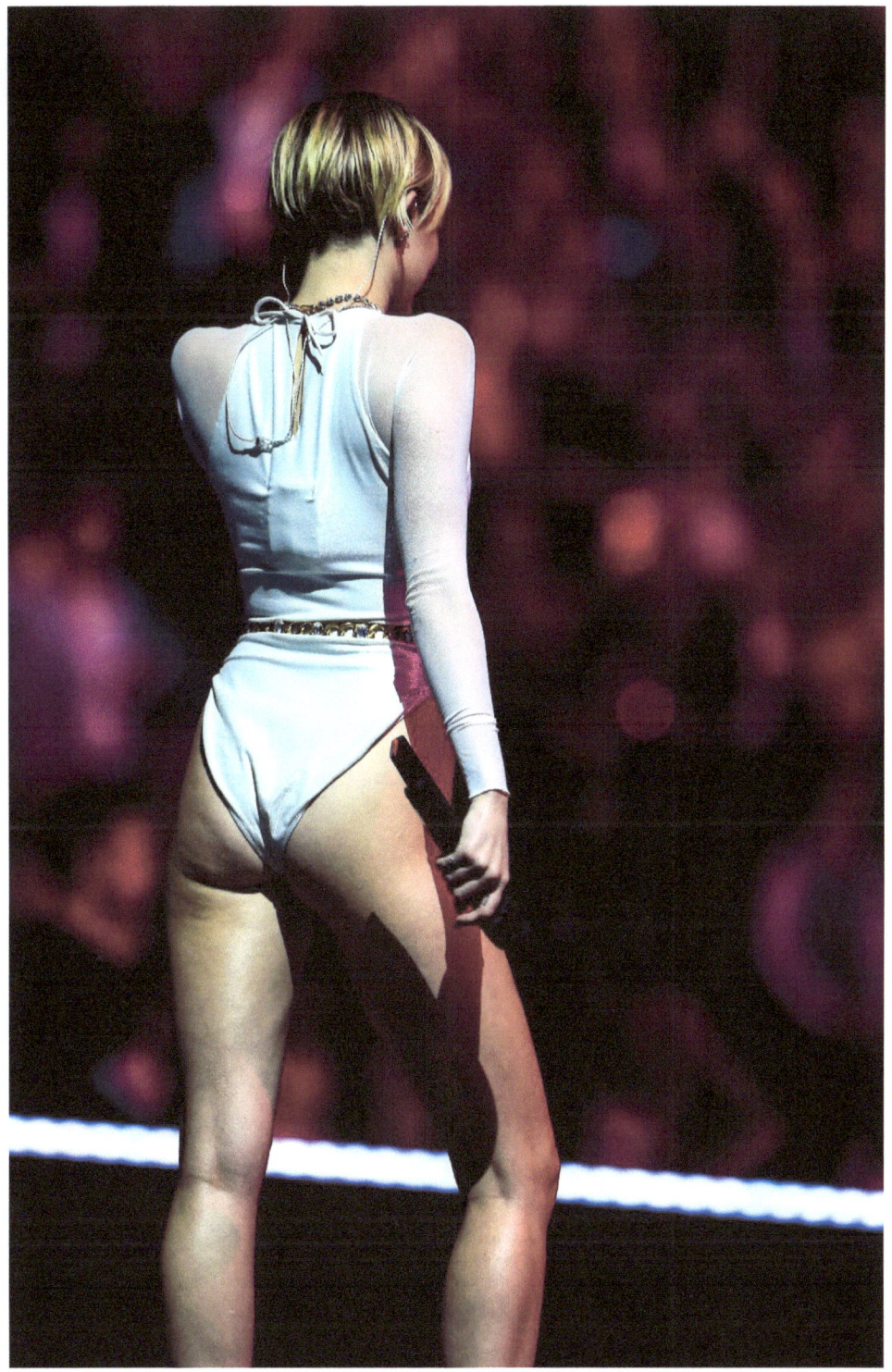

Miley ray Cyrus "The Little Girl Who Grew Into A Woman"

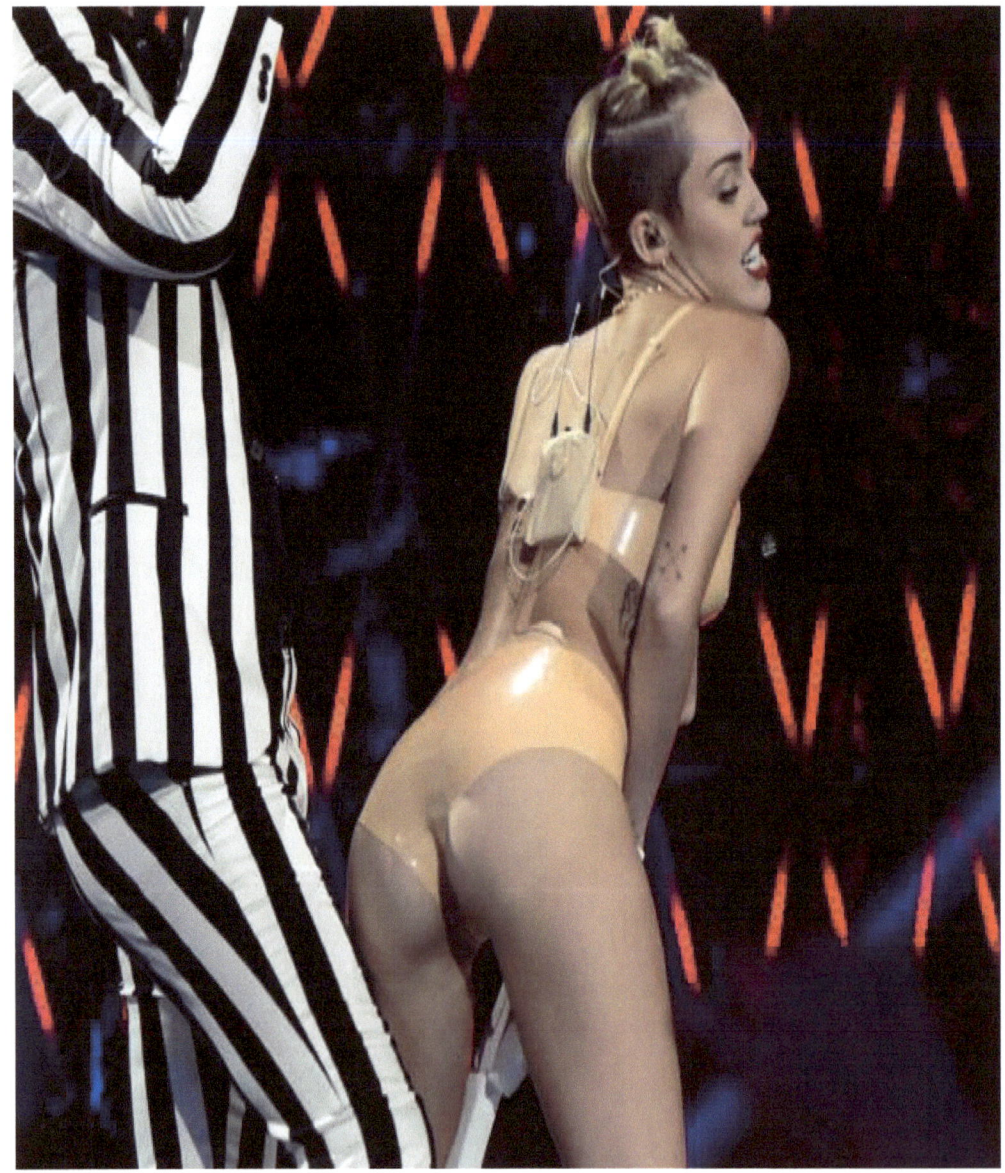

Miley ray Cyrus "The Little Girl Who Grew Into A Woman"

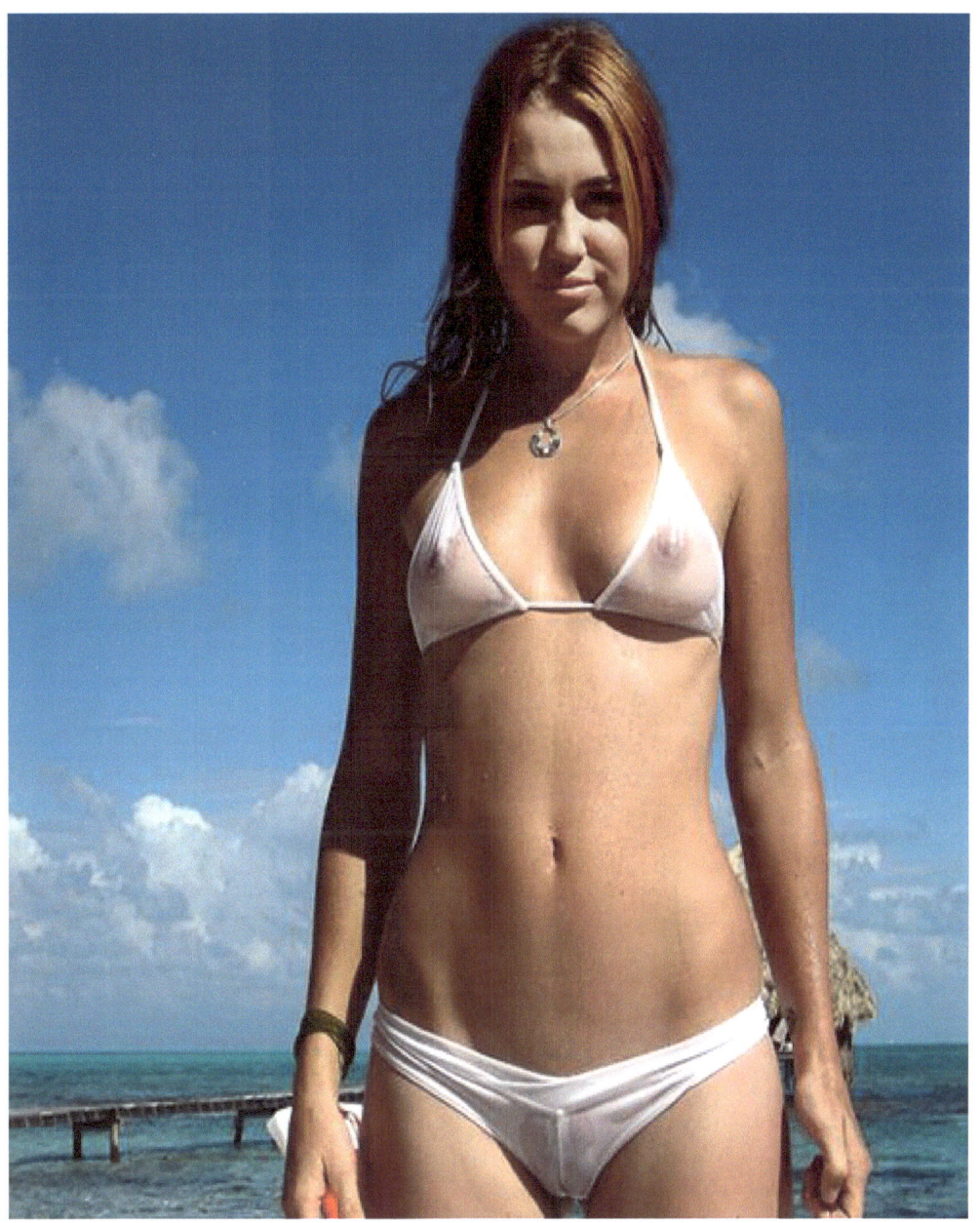

Miley ray Cyrus "The Little Girl Who Grew Into A Woman"

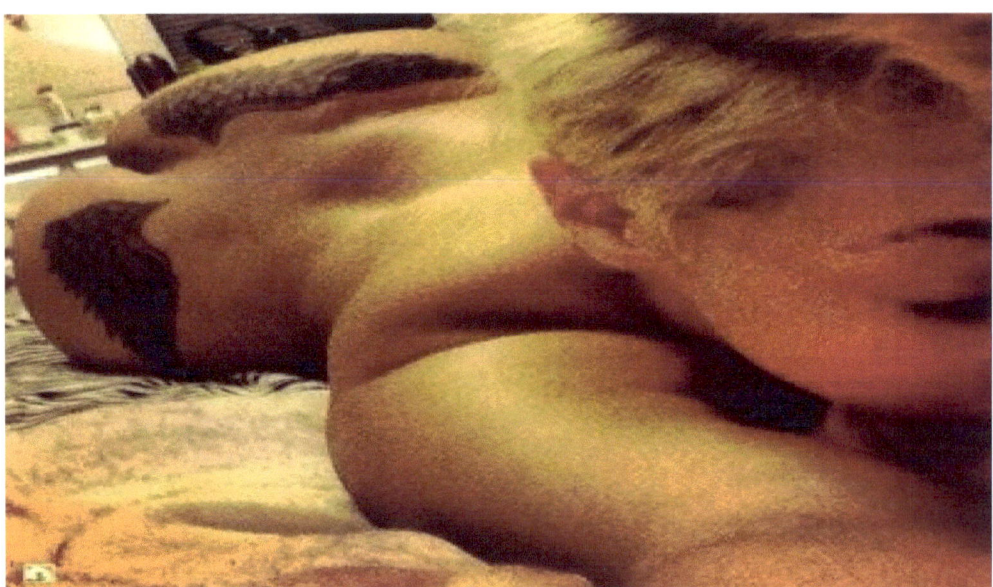

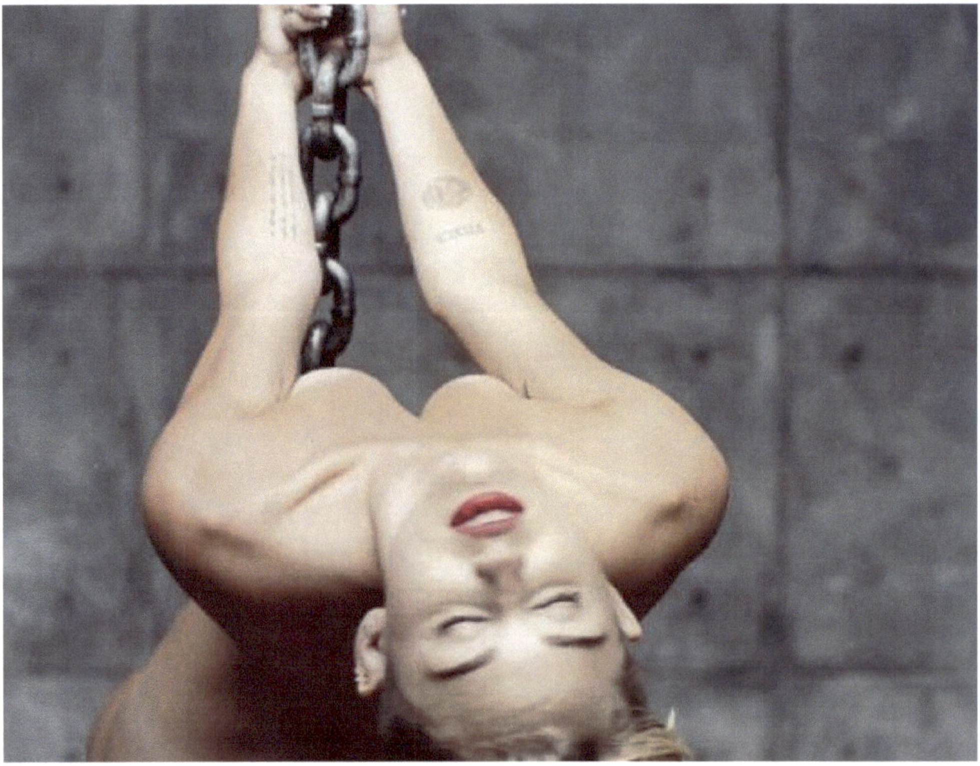

Miley ray Cyrus "The Little Girl Who Grew Into A Woman"

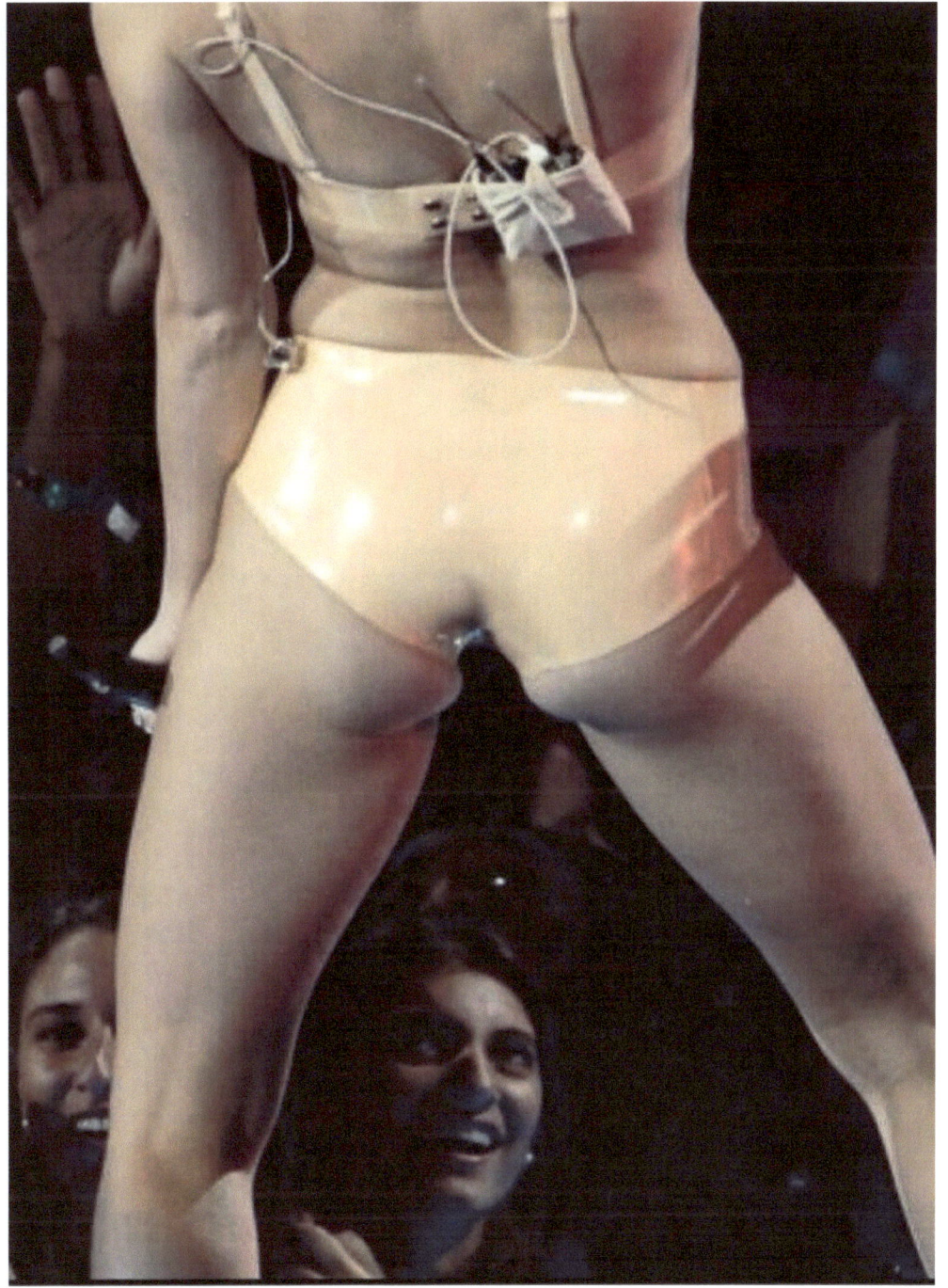

Miley ray Cyrus "The Little Girl Who Grew Into A Woman"

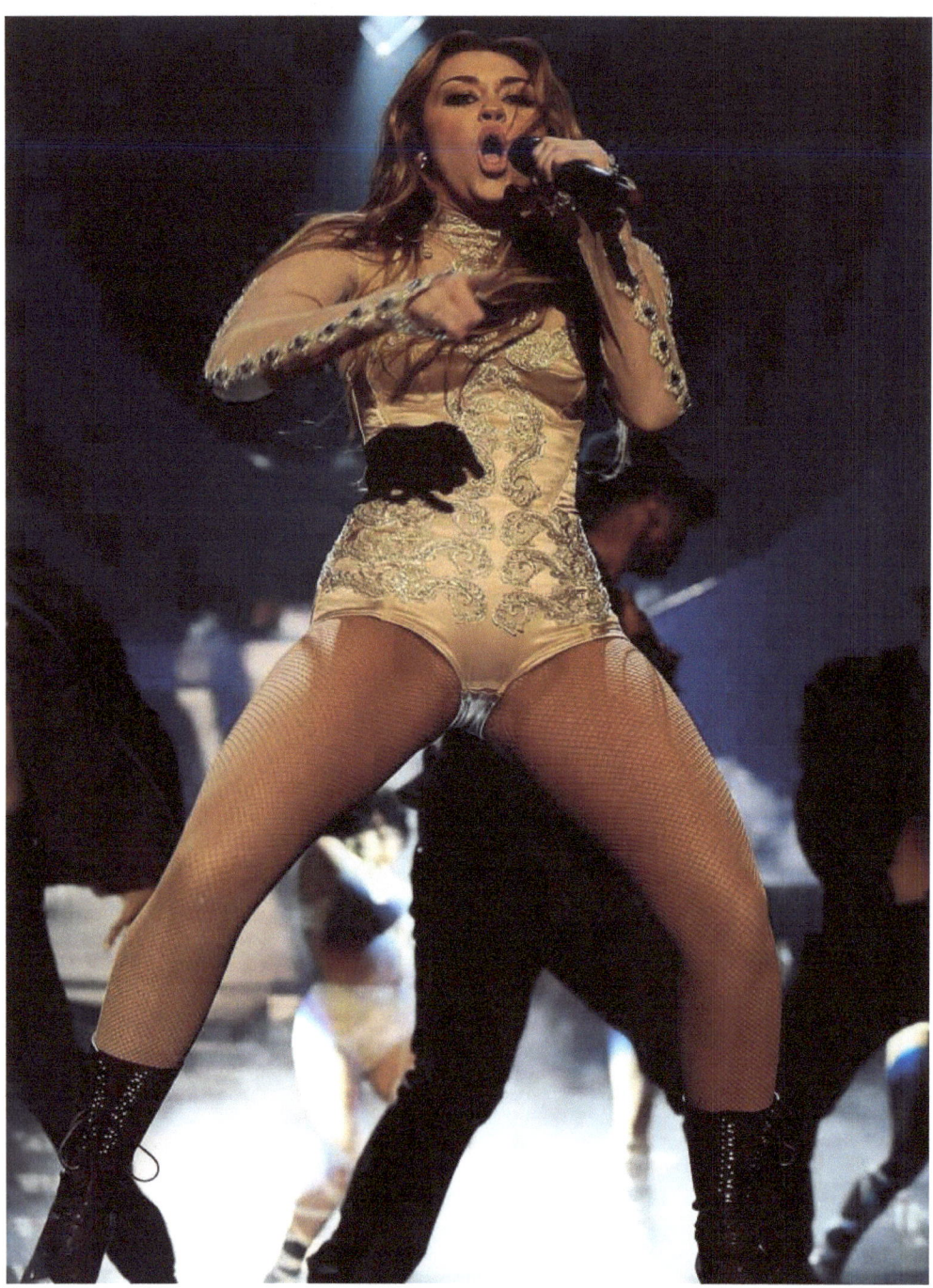

Miley ray Cyrus "The Little Girl Who Grew Into A Woman"

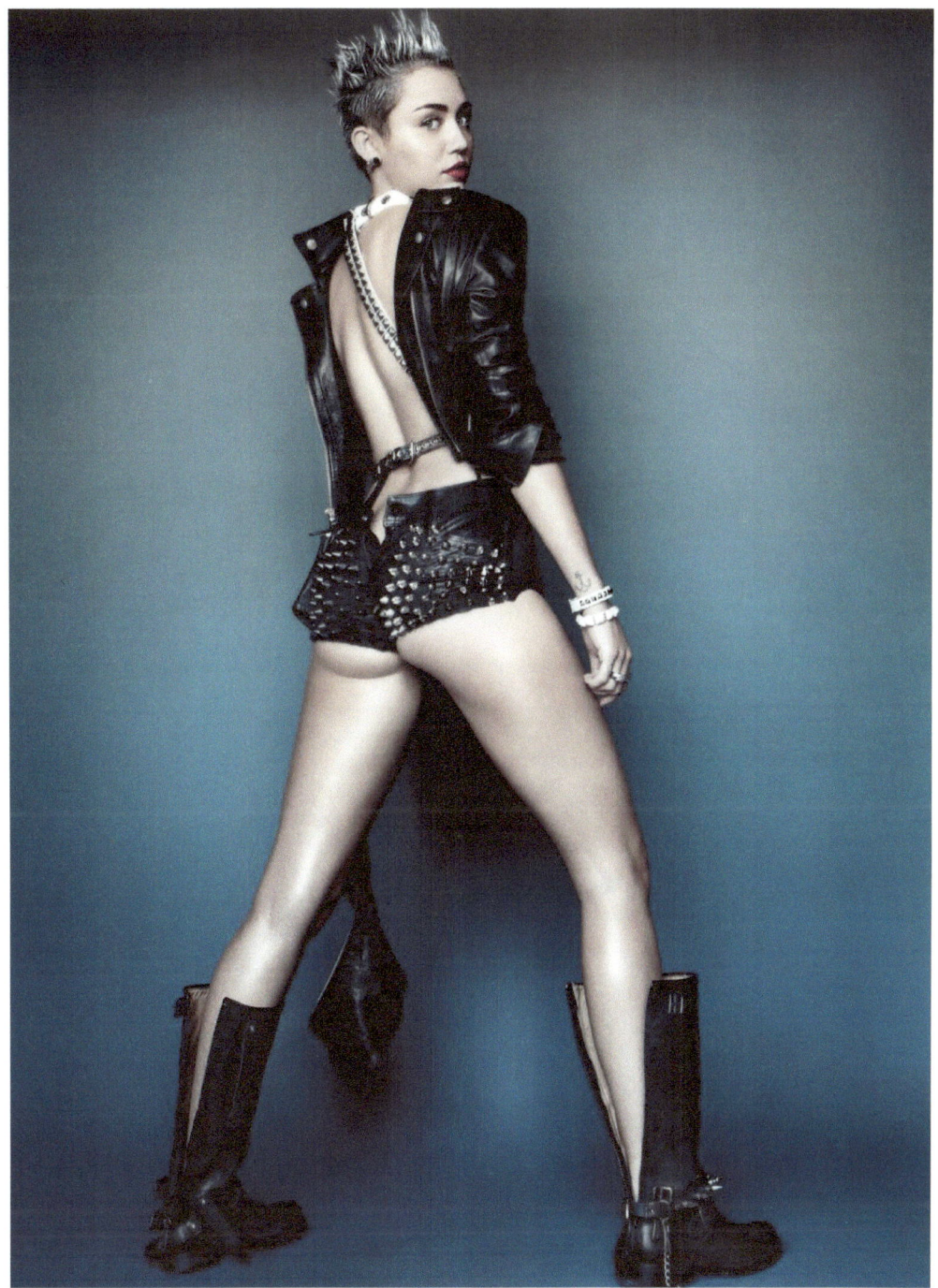

Miley ray Cyrus "The Little Girl Who Grew Into A Woman"

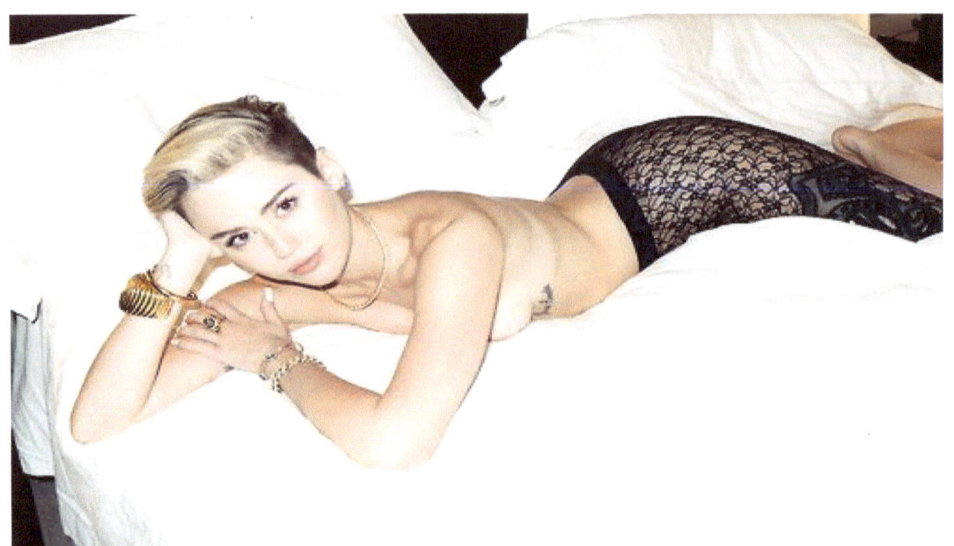

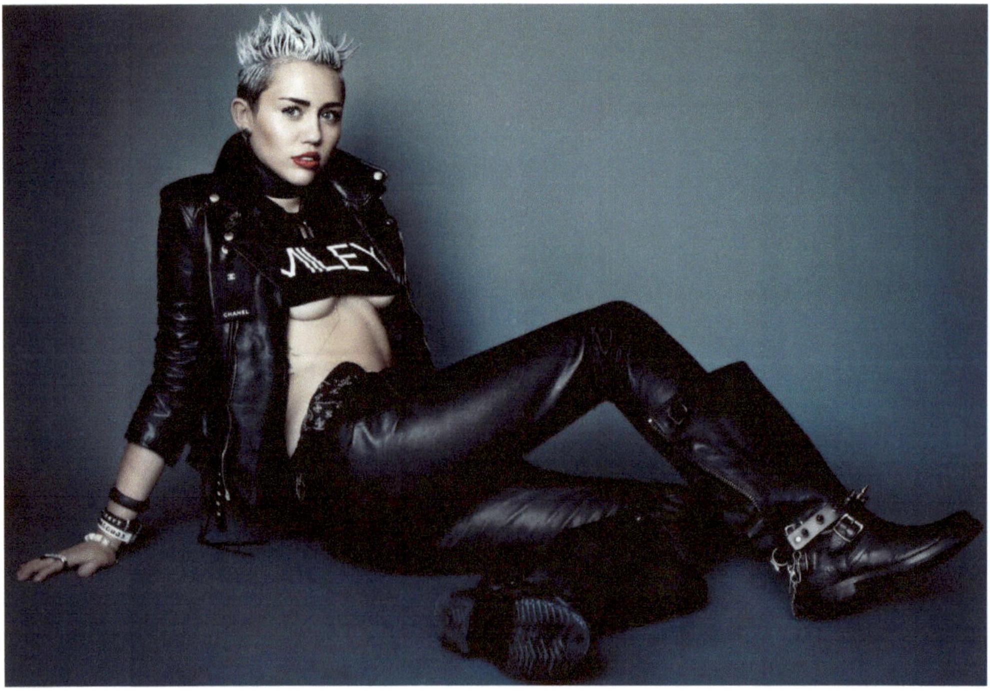

Miley ray Cyrus "The Little Girl Who Grew Into A Woman"

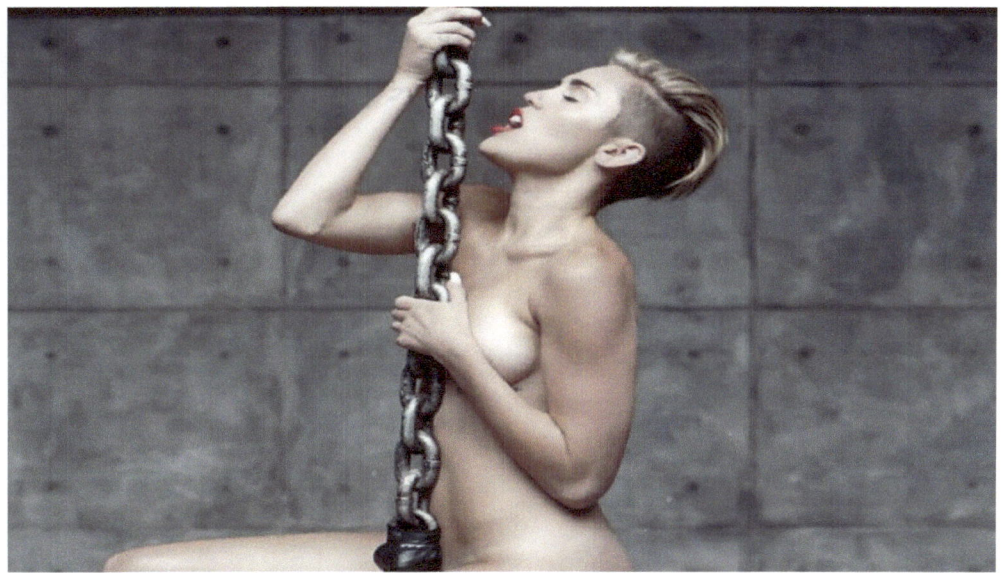

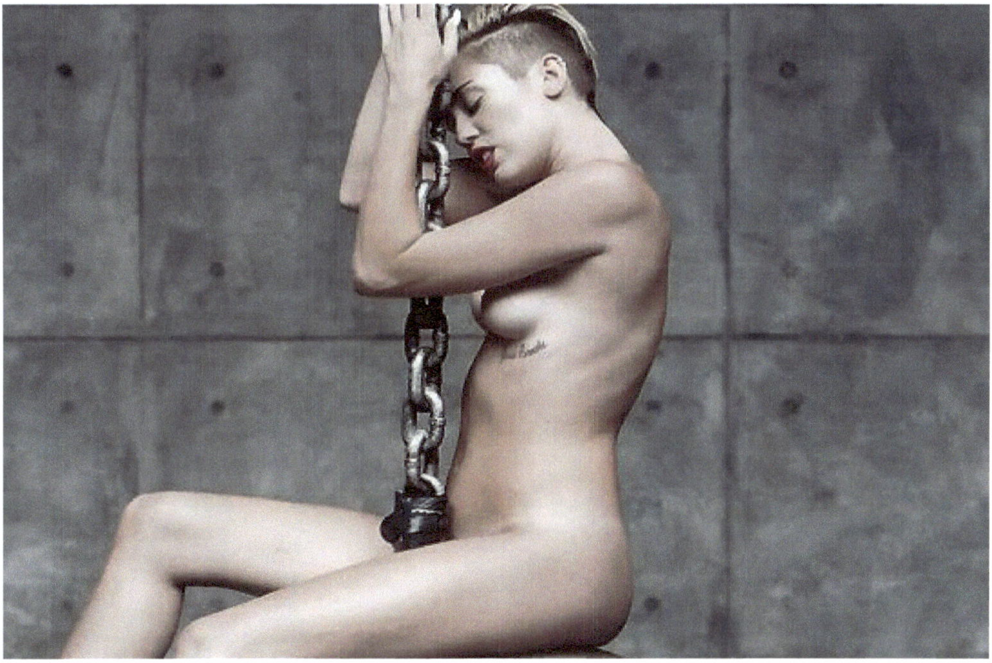

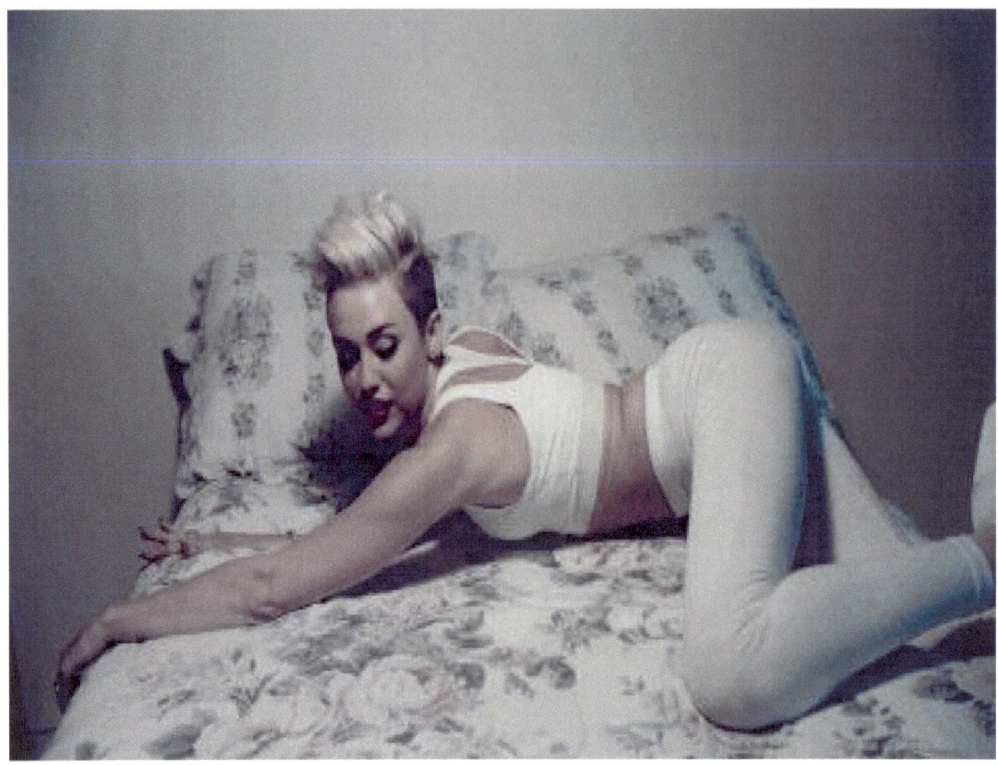

Miley "SEXY" Ray Cyrus!